First Blood

Natalie D-Napoleon
First Blood

For my baba, Ivica, and all the unseen girls

First Blood
ISBN 978 1 76041 776 5
Copyright © text Natalie D-Napoleon 2019
Cover artwork: Kathryn Morrison
Cover design: Brett Leigh Dicks

First published 2019 by
GINNINDERRA PRESS
PO Box 3461 Port Adelaide 5015 Australia
www.ginninderrapress.com.au

Contents

Sometimes I Need to Say Less	7
Grains of Sand	8
Stories & Sand	9
Questions	12
Domestic Life	15
Black Swan	16
Educating a Girl	19
The Swallows in the Shed	21
Carrots	23
Bhreus	25
Dert Rendezvous	28
How to Make Sand	29
The Peppermint Tree	30
My Little	31
I'd See Patterns	32
Short Skirts	33
First Blood: A Sestina	34
At a Girl	36
A Kind of Breaking	37
Zemlja	39
Definition: Wog (n); a Thing	41
Pioneer Day	44
No Box	46
Family History	49
I Hear Things	50
The Mouth is a Door	51
Careful	54
Come Walk With Me	56
Fake Plastic Plants	57
You Say Poetry is Dead	59

In the Night Wood	61
My Body is a Poem	62
o o O	63
Your Mother Says it Was the Books	64
Mother Cento	66
The First Drug	67
Bird Song	70
Acknowledgements	71
References and Notes	72
Thanks	74

Sometimes I Need to Say Less

Sometimes I need to say
                 less
to make a poem work,
sometimes more.
Sometimes,
it feels like
there are
one hundred words
in my mouth
for every grain
of sand on earth,
and at the same time
there are never enough,
never enough,
to say all the things
that need to be said.

Grains of Sand

Oh!   the
                 wind wept

The
             far off

Far away
                     a friend

     of fire

Stories & Sand

I can never remember / the first time / I learnt
stepping / on a double gee / with bare feet /
stings / then itches / then stings / then
itches / again / and again / and again

But I will never / forget / to look down /
whenever / wearing bare feet / for the three-cornered / jack /
the creeping limbs / of the prostrate plant herbaceous /
green and soft as clover / when blooming /
lying in wait in camouflage / on the West Australian dirt /
sand brown and / sharp / as devil's horns when spent

The song lines tell us / we connect /
through the stories we share /
we connect / because every
Aussie child has / stepped on
a prickle / or a thorn / or a double gee
still and golden brown /– kids know
what it means / to be barefoot
and free –

The '-ologies' / and the '-istics' / and the '-alities' /
and the '-tions' of Man / escape me / endlessly / like numbers
like musical notes / on a page / like being in the
tomb of an Egyptian pharaoh / plundered of everything /
except the palimpsest / of hieroglyphs / thousands of
years old / not knowing / what they mean
stripped bare of the '-ologies' / and '-istics' / and '-alities'
and '-tions' / of hu- / mans

In the end / all that matters / is dis-
covery / digging in the dirt / because
everything is / stories & sand /
stories & sand /

To find the gap / the crack that
Leonard Cohen sings / lets the light in /
is a place to begin /
And to / dis- / cover / and to write /
to write / in the coal mine / is the light
insisting / its way through the / crack /
that lights up the / pathway /
to dis- / covery / dis- / covery

If I could begin again / I would still
wander barefoot / as a child
I would choose / to take a chance / to step
on those devil's thorns /
If I could smell again / the bush after rain /
hear the frogs / call me to sleep /
and step for a moment / in the skin / of an / Other

If I could begin again / I would
stamp / into a molten coin /
'surrender' on one side / and 'humility' on the other /
then keep the coin / in my pocket /
turn it over / in my fingers / heating
the metal from cold / to warm / in my hands
keeping it warm / by my thigh

Then I would put on / the coal miner's hat /
click the torch on / take off my boots
and / get to work /
deep down /
deep down /
to the stories / to the dirt.

Questions

There was one question
then another, and another;
the child was full of
questions, questions.

there was the crunching
of feet on the brick pavers
laid out in a herringbone
pattern, fish bones

feed the mother's ferns
growing in the shade
of the patio,
the mother and child

cleaning the sliding glass
windows of the double-
brick farmhouse
with Windex blue as sky.

The mother wipes in
swift, strong, circular
strokes, and the child
tried to copy her – or so

I imagine – the girl was
five and full of five
year-old questions
about poop and stars and

why ants walk in single
file, and then she made
a statement,
'Mummy, I know why

you're a Mum
because you're so
good at cooking
and cleaning.'

The mother stops
mid-stroke, clouds
of white foam in
an unfinished circle

on the glass.
Whose voice was
the girl speaking with?
The foam drips,

a sob escapes
the mother's mouth, then
she runs inside the house,
the sliding glass

door snapping shut behind
her like a slap. The girl has no
idea, no idea what she has
said. She only knows

the cleaning of the
glass sliding doors
is not finished yet
and the dust, the dust

keeps coming, like
the questions,
like the Easterlies
that blow in

from the Wheatbelt
and don't stop
until they reach
the ocean.

Domestic Life

        easily defined

          domestic life

isolate

      a house

           master   servant

         sublimation of self,

                          I

would have endured anything

          the house   quiet,   the sil-

ver dish,

                ignorance.
      The   restlessness of my girl-

hood   gone.

Black Swan

I pluck from my
ribs one black feather
then another three
arise in its place,
like feeding bread
to the black swans with
my father as a child
at Bibra Lake, ripping
off one chunk brings
a bank of swans; a
magnet through the
sand to attract iron ore.
My shoulders itch,
spines of feathers
spiking through skin.
I flap my arms, not yet
ready to fly. The Noongar
throw a handful of sand
into a body of water,
speak language,
let the Waugal
know we are here.
Now, we live in a time
of the Mass Forgetting.
Now, bulldozers come
to scrape and wrench
the earth clean for
another road-to-nowhere,

road-to-nowhere, road-
to-nowhere... Fists full
of sand pour into the lake
but there is no ceremony,
only the low din and vibration
of con-struction/de-struction.
I remain the good wife;
I whistle to my cygnets,
I flap my wings three times,
honk and hiss at the
golden demon –
rara avis in terris
nigroque simillima
cygno – a rare bird
in the earth very much
like a black swan.
My fleshy lips turn
into a keratin-skin bill,
flag red, a memory:
eagles wrenching
arrogant white feathers;
falling, falling, falling.
A sepulchral cloak of
black loaned from
a saviour of ravens.

The white tips remain
on my wings, tracks of
my fall marked by stars of
flannel flowers. *Kooldjak,
gooldjak, maali;* you will call
my name. Even if you deny
my existence I continue to be
a wedge of obsidian wings
beating beneath the
land's surface.

Kooldjak, gooldjak, maali – words for swan of Noongar peoples from the south-west of Western Australia

Educating a Girl

It smelled like dust, insubstantial, yet heavy
with having missed out, once again,
on what the boys were doing –
running down the track
(vegetables swaying on either side of me)
behind the beaten Toyota ute, where the paint
had peeled off, the rust flickering red in the sun.
A face full of dust, gasping.

It tasted like metal in my mouth as I bit
into the side of my cheek and the blood
leaked into the cracks between my gums and teeth.
At school, on the radio, on the TV,
they told us girls could do anything,
be anything that boys could be.
On the radio Cyndi Lauper sang,
'Girls just wanna have fu-uun' –
at home us girls were told
to hold on to our pee on long car rides.
I press my face against the safety-logo-tattooed
car window while my brothers pee,
free, standing up, on the side of the road
because girls can hold on, but boys can't.
A fishhook mouth, bleeding.

It felt like sandpaper under my fingers
while trying to read Braille.
It felt like a vice on my lungs,
the one my dad had on his workbench
in the shed, the one he used to repair
the irrigation pipes, bending them
back into shape after the tractor
hoe had hacked them up.
A hand full of sand, grasping.

It looked like rust red flickering in the sun
my dad and my brothers
return from the fishing trip, and me,
his daughter, chewing on the dust, my teeth
squeaking and crunching on the sand's uneven
beads, my hunger unsatisfied, the moisture
taken from my mouth. 'Hold on, hold on,'
they continue to say while the blood
pools in our mouths, and sandpaper pads –
'But all I wanted to do was
go fishing with the boys.'

The Swallows in the Shed

The swallows
in the shed
leave a circle
of white, Pollock-like
bird crap stains
on the vein-cracked
concrete floor.
Every spring,
with mud and
spit and the
warm air of
wishes
they make
a new nest
tucked into
the most silent
corner of the shed,
where even
the redback
spiders vacate,
away from
the wheeze and splutter
of the Massey Ferguson
and the clawing
arms of four
curious kids.
Every spring the
black and orange
chicks' mouths

open in
hungry prayer,
the shit stain
art appears,
dries up and crusts,
then disappears,
swept up with
a thick, bristled
broom, scraped
away with
the piles of sand
out the door
to summer.

Carrots

I

Carrots, naranče orange,
covered in their down-like root threads
tumble and tumble in the washer- barrel,
through 600 gallons of water – the barrel
invented by some Spearwood wog to clean
the carrots of soil-sand-grit before they went
to market. Hours before, we had swum in that
water, four farm kids cooling off in the high
heat. Sometimes, we'd help pick carrots with
a twist-pull-snap, twist-pull-snap, once
or twice we would twist-pull-snap from
the earth two carrots locked in a last
embrace, like two people found in
Pompeii entwined under 1700
years of ash and sand, the me-
mory of an original rain-
bow palette of carrot
colours, purple black
white yellow reddish
faded like clothes
left on the Hill's
Hoist for
week-
s in
the
su
n
.

II

After being spat on
and wiped on shorts, baby
carrots taste milky when they-
're first picked and eaten; grains
of sand squeaking teeth – and if
you eat enough baby carrots in a
competition with your brothers,
neighbour and sister, your stomach
will clench and you'll have to rush
to the loo. Yesterday, I bought
carrots packaged in a clear
body-bag at the un-Super-
market, took out a single
carrot, spat on it, wip-
ed it on my shirt
and took a bite;
it was woody,
the skin bitter
& dry – like the
couple in Pom-
peii locked in a
timeless em-
brace only
a trace of
what on-
ce was
rem-
ain-
ed
.

Bhreus

i sprout and swell
like a wild wolf cub

like an unfurling kangaroo paw
like a stone

breast buds hurt
to sleep on

there's the shame
like lying on two marbles

beneath my blue-veined chest
rivulets of blood vessels

branch out to supply
the growing adipose tissue

my cousin's fiancé
stares at my buds –

sitting across from me
at our fake wood veneer dining table

the plastic beginning to curl
at the edges – as they swell

beneath my spaghetti-strap tank top
and i feel bloody and raw

as a flank steak
invented as a woman

as i am observed
the shame of adults

watching a wild thing
grow untamed yet contained

why can't flowers bloom
in the dark?

why can't wolf cubs
raise themselves?

but there's no blooming
in the dark or hunting pups.

carnivorous plant eyes
eating my breast buds

i have eyes on my areola
hypnotising and dark pink

as lips above and below
like a target my nipples

as enveloping as a pupil
dark as a pool of black ink –

i don't eat anything
with an eye –

but I am not an
'I'

i am
just a girl

just a girl
just a girl bud

with breast buds
better to plant my

feet in a field of dirt
and let the sun adore me

than to stand in
here in the cool air

and allow myself to
be potted and pruned

and planted and put
in a box to be eaten

by eyes/Is/ayes.

Dert Rendezvous

        cities clatter
          haunts of
    secret
        land

              a silver

    cry

A trail of sand
          all   is swept
Clean

   my   rendezvous
    moon

How to Make Sand

First, a star must be formed;
bodies colliding into hot bodies;

through infinite time and space
destroying one story, creating another,

molten ball of fire and gas
time upon time, and when that fire dies out,

or retreats deep into the core
Earth, the planet, and earth, the terra, is made.

Then, take a rock or a mountain or a hill
wear it down, wear it down.

Rocks broken back and forth through time;
epiclastic: storms, water, wind,

the moon's pull, the tides,
clocks that curl under the earth's beach;

shaping, until it is between two millimetres
and a sixteenth of a millimetre, not so

round or perfect or thin.
Silica and quartz, gypsum, coral

and shell, obsidian grains, deep olivine –
zircon, 4.4 billion years old,

found in the Jack Hills of Western Australia,
on earth for 98 per cent of its existence,

and still you call this a new land.

The Peppermint Tree

When I was a child how I loved, how I loved, how I loved a tree,
I sang my troubles to her and she hummed her leaf-buzz tune in return.
A peppermint, catching the breeze in a skirt of finger leaves,
Swishing and rustling, songs stuck like feathers to a berm.
Irresistible, to reach and crush and inhale one spear-leaf's biting scent,
Stabbing into my jeans, like a lock of hair slipped into a lover's pocket,
An elixir of sorts, a language of the senses, knowing but never meant.
'What about me?' I sang, and you gave more than I put into that pocket.
Surprise-attack seeds thrown like pellets of laughter between siblings,
A place to hide away from my mother's raised voice, the red unfriend.
At the foot of your trunk, nursed back to life, a fledgling,
Feeding me minced meat by hand, till I found my strength again.
You were a mother's dress for a child to hide underneath,
While I took from you a handful of seeds and a leaf, a leaf, a leaf.

My Little

                a little
        somewhere in the West –

                a nice grassy
                stretch

 cool   thirst

Waters

                still

                        my heart

                                  azure

my
somewhere in the West

I'd See Patterns

I'd see patterns everywhere 　　　　　　　handwriting
nests
　uneasy　　　lace　　I dreamed
　　　　unraveled
　　　　　　　like a web. My hands
　　　　　　　　　　　a stranger.

　　　　　　　　　　　books to my room

　　　　　　　　a
　　　　　　　　　friendly

　　　　　　　　　death.

　　　　　　　the carcasses of small birds

　　　　　　　　　　princess
　　　　　　　black magic　　refused
　　　　　　　　　little corpses

Short Skirts

The mother marches over to her / while she's playing
and giggling / with her cousins / boys / and / girls / hisses
just loud enough / for her to hear / 'I've told you /
before / good girls / keep their legs / closed' /
She is thirteen / the first buds / of her breasts like pimples
of embarrassment / rising on her chest / But it's not
her fault / the mother is right / she is always right /
girls that spread their legs / in miniskirts are
sluts / and she needs / to keep her legs / shut / shut / shut //

Her mother was / protecting / her / from all the dugites /
and tiger snakes / that slither through the banksias /
and wheat-coloured rye grass / hiding under the
rust-stained corrugated iron / dumped in the bush next door /
The snake is never to blame / a predator lying in wait /
an ouroboros curled / in a spiral / at the foot of a Tuart tree /
shedding its cage / swallowing its own tail / the end
is the beginning / the beginning is the end //

And why / is the first woman / who grabbed the first /
pomegranate / dropped it / then watched
it split / open / like an atom / open to infinity /
the first drops / falling / a red stain /
never to leave her hands / to blame
when behind her / Adam was whispering /
'You go first / pick it / take a bite'? /
She thought she / would watch / the world open up – /
'Trust me' he said / complete the circle /
spill the first blood / make it all right /
but be sure to / close / your legs / real
tight / short skirts / are the end /
and the beginning / you know //

First Blood: A Sestina

There was a time when the girl
never thought about the colour blue, or blood,
could be amused by the flicking of a lit match,
the delicate shiver of a spider orchid;
summer holidays stretched out, days dropping time
like a missed knitting stitch.

But her body was not hers, a stitch
of animal, a pinch of dirt, a girl
is made of words plus liquid minus time
and what she does not have; blood,
defines her. Like an orchid
about to bloom she unfurls, unlit match

between her teeth, nobody to match
her unkissed lips, until the stitch
is pulled and the thread of the cloth orchid
undoes, just enough to reveal the gone girl.
Nobody told her there would be so much blood!
Her mother had tried to mend the old time

ways, when girls were never told in time
about periods, as if knowledge alone could match
an image of her *baba* scrubbing the blood
out of torn rags, her hair greasy, a stitch
unwashed once every month. Cold water, girls
know, washes out blood, and orchids

should be kept indoors and warm, orchids
are to be protected from a cold breeze. In time
the blue liquid in the TV ads for girl-
products made sense, red stains to mismatch
the pastel spots on her skirt enough to stitch
shame to her chest. Blood

is not to be seen – except the blood
of war or violence. Blood 'n Bone drinks the orchid,
the fetor forcing the girl to sprint until a stitch
bites her side and the breath of time
stabs; finding a way to strike the match
of bloom and decay in the body of a girl.

She came to see a stitch in time
    could not repair the stain of first blood, spider orchids
are too delicate to touch, and nothing can hold a match to a
    bleeding girl.

At a Girl

                dust, insubstantial

            boys
running down the track

                rust flickering red in the sun. A
face full of dust

his daughter, chewing
        crunching on   sand's uneven beads,   hunger

tasted like metal
          blood
Leaks into the cracks
   school   told us girls
          be

                  but boys can't
                  bleed

          bending
     into shape

rust red flickering in the sun.

A Kind of Breaking

Kindness is a kind of breaking,
the smell of burnt iron, a tarnished
silver ring surrounding a heart,
a gift at seven years of age
from a boychild, with eyes as bright
sky as the bird on the ring, hair golden
and shining like Jason with his fleece.

He wasn't like the gang of boys
who followed me singing KISS songs,
'Ca-a-an-dy tonight's the night for lovin,'
and when I would turn to take notice,
'Suck-hole smartass you think
you're too good for us but you stink.'
Until I broke down – oh, but I wanted
them to 'like' me! Like; a palindrome
of feelings, meaning the same
thing backwards as it does forwards –
a girl couldn't be all things,
so I had to be put in my girl
place, with my girl face;
emotional and stretched,
like a wool cloth on tenterhooks,
drying in the iris-burning Perth sun –
wanting to shrink – yet held fast
in the frame. And where was Jason,
out catching gold in the river
with his fleece?

Years later, the child's bluebird ring on my
right-hand pinky finger, expanded
and dented, to remind me of
stretching-breaking-open,
because I would not shrink for them,
because I would not break.

Zemlja

I am the coloniser
and the colonised.
The *zemlja*,
an egg-timer filled with
beads of sand, blood and *kiša*
that I cannot hold or contain,
runs through my fingers.

I sprint through the freshly rotary-hoed bed
the sand-searing February coals,
my feet sinking up to my ankles
like poofing through silken powder,
or a virgin snow fall I have never known.
I stop – 'Is three minutes all I have
before I burn to dust, to glass?'

My feet could be the roots
of a sprouting seed, pressed into
the soil with an index finger,
the blue beads of NPK fertiliser and
butterfly sprinklers rusty red
coaxing me to grow
from deep below,
from under,
from the bore,
from the pre-human aquifer,
but they will never be –

I am a seedling
plucked from my mother's womb
the spongy organ of the placenta
entwined within
the tendrils of my
embryonic roots,
transplanted into
the sandy sandy sand sand
to grow devotional
to the *zemlja* of a
Western land.

A foreign land,
a foreign sand.
My land. My sand.
An Other's land.
Outside
(and inside),
Other and all,
coloniser and colonised –

I sprint four strides
'poof poof – poof poof'
across the ploughed bed,
into the shade, before
the 4 p.m. sun turns me to dust –

zemlja (Croatian) – earth, soil, land, dirt, ground and country. Pronounced ze'mlya /ˈzɛːmlja/.
kiša (Croatian) – rain

Definition: Wog (n); a Thing

A wog is a word for a thing
a polliwog, a golliwogg
a black-face doll –
a sailor who has not
crossed the equator –
with a halo of hair and
a gash of lips, no hips, frozen
in time, a white minstrel
thing, a caricature –
a word from the past
not used anymore.

A golliwogg is a doll,
a story, created by Florence K. Up-
ton and illustrated –
a face on jam and Blackjack
confection – a children's toy,
a ploy of affectation, not
affection – a germ, bug, infection
or illness of the gut –
something you don't
want to have or be. 'Pick
her or him, not me, not me.'

A wog is not Working
On Government Service,
a wog is not a Western
Oriental Gentleman,
worthy, wily or wonderful,
a W.O.G is not an acronym.
A wog is a word for a thing.
A wog is a scattermouch,
it is Indian, Arab, Asian,
a wog is a word used for post-World War II
Southern-European immigration.

A wog is not out of work,
a wog is not a boy. Greeks,
Italians, Croatians and
Portuguese use the word
with ease that was once
a racial slur. You get a rise
out of not knowing
where you come from
anymore. A wog was my *baba*
and *deda*, my brothers,
father, mother and sister.

A wog belongs to the Empire,
and an Empire likes a wog
that is cheap and for hire,
'The wogs begin at Calais' –
and they become a *parle*,
refugees, fresh off the boat
people, queue jumpers, r/evolving,
speak *Inglese*, speak illegalese –
a wog becomes a sailor
who has crossed
the equator.

baba (Croatian) – grandmother
deda (Croatian) – grandfather

Pioneer Day

Once I was a wilderness,
a poor common farmer,
a pioneer myth to take
you anywhere, as I
strummed the love songs
to be property, married,
my mouth pressed against
the wind of the first settlers free.

Once I was a Tuart seedling
planted on Western Australia's 150th year,
a tongue controlled
with trinkets shiny.
Aboriginal peoples in chains
a hiccup of history,
enslaved by the song
from the blue guitar.

Once I was a stick
with beer bottle caps,
hanging off the boat,
a farm out the back.
Damper, a communion
wafer, stuck like glue
to the roof of my mouth,
on Pioneer Day at school.

Once I was six ribbons
to tie back your lips blue,
servants to a rare dirt,
a tune that we share.
Empire-soaked feats
unmoored by children,
sunburnt faces adrift,
grains of sand in the scree.

No Box

I used to say,
'My *baba* speaks
broken English,'
but now I know
my English
         is
     bro
              ken.

I found out
recently
I spoke
an Other
language
as a child,
a language
that I cannot
speak now.

I think that
is why I continue
to say
'spill'
the spoilt milk
down the sink,

instead of
'tip' –
the tongue of
the mother
imprinted
like the smell
of breast milk
on an infant.

When I used
to fill out
those forms,
those
government forms,
'Do you speak
a language
other than
English
at home?'
There was
no box
to tick for
'Used to speak
another language
as a child.'

Tick – No other language at home.
Tick – English.

No box for,
'Parents used to
speak Croatian
at home
but stopped
because their
children told them
to speak
English,
because
they were
embarrassed,
because
they didn't
want to be
different
from the
other
kids.'

No box
for that.

Family History

She used to wear miniskirts and drive a red Mini. He used to spray DDT because it gave his dad headaches. He left school at 14, 12 years later she left school at 14 as well. Her father said girls didn't need an education. He was the only son of five children. He told his children a Rhodes scholar used to copy his work at school. His four children rolled their eyes at him. The grandfather pulled him out of high school after one year to run the family farm. The Dad said the only reason he left home at 33 was because of the miniskirt. The 21-year-old long, brown legs agreed. There was a lamb on the spit, stuffed with onions and garlic. There was necking in the car at the King's Park lookout. A wig and a June wedding, fur cuffs on the bridesmaid's sleeves, bags of sugared almonds. Two Yugoslav families each glad to find one of their own. There was a fresh concrete pad and a house on Hotspur Road less than a mile from his parent's house; a lawnmowing job, an inheritance, then a return to the farm work. There was an *Encyclopedia Britannica* read from A to Z. There were two people working in the fields six days a week, cabbage ice creams for the kids and dugites in the cucumbers. There was a surgery to strip the varicose veins on the long, brown legs. There was a litter of rabbits buried in the carrots by the father's hand. At the father's funeral the Rhodes scholar came up to the eldest daughter and told her how he used to copy off her dad at school. He told her how he had such a brain. How he could have done anything with his life. This time, she didn't roll her eyes.

I Hear Things

                                          I hear   things

              sneaking

True

                                      one small

                fool's   opportunity

  – to work *hard* –

        To

                                  sur-

vive this midnight entry. On
      earth

                raking,   scrubbing
           stitching

                                        bent back.

The Mouth is a Door

The mouth is a door,
a pop and burst
as I strip a stalk
of seedless Thompson
baby grapes
in my mouth at the
Farmer's Market.
A sweet welcome on
the tip of my tongue,
bitter skin slides
down the lazy flesh
of my tongue's sides
telescoping me back
to the grapes growing
on the trellis
by the waves
of the asbestos fence
in my *baba*'s backyard,
the ones she
pollinated by hand
sacrificing
one bunch
of grape flowers
to brush against
all the others
open with
promise.

During the school
year my *deda*
tended the gardens
of Guildford Grammar School,
kids in shirts and ties
called him 'wog'
and, maybe, he called them
'red-faced *Inglese*'
under his breath.
He came from a country
where he'd been
Italian, British,
Austro-Hungarian
and Yugoslav
in his lifetime,
but in this country
he would always be
one thing, from
somewhere else.

In my grandparents' hometown,
on the island of Korčula,
nobody knows
how long grapes
have been grown
and cultivated;
is it 2,000 or 2,500 years?
And who even knew
what the Illyrians grew

before the Greeks
and Italians, then Slavs
came to take
their land?

As the family moved
into the red
double-brick house
in the suburbs,
the backyard trellis
of grapes
was abandoned
for the pinpricks of roses
and the paper cuts
of buffalo grass,
the grape vines
left to the *baba*s
and *deda*s
to maintain,
keeping that door
open
a crack.

Careful

Squid ink risotto dark as the depths of the Mediterranean Sea; handmade gnocchi that dissolve in the mouth; lamb neck, cabbage and fennel stew, sharp and astringent to a seven-year-old's tongue; whole lamb on the spit, turning, waiting, cracked peppercorns, garlic salt and onion, fat that melts and spits, spits, spits, made with my mother's hands, my father's hands, salt, garlic stuffed into the flank, onions overflowing from the cavity where the stomach once was. Flaky, powdery twisted bliss a thousand Venetian years in one crisp-fried pastry *hrustule*. *Kiflici*, shortbread biscuits, curved Ottoman quarter moons, a brief rule of delight. Cobbler stew, flesh that melts, made with potatoes and onions and garlic – in shallow night water, the price of a cobbler barb in my father's bare foot. 'Keep peeling garlic until you think you've peeled enough, then peel some more.' Snapper fish-head soup, creamy, sodium, rice absorbing the dense goodness of the flavours of the fish head and bones, topped with fresh flat leaf parsley from the home garden – 'Eat carefully around the gut, child' – olive oil and garlic, whole fish over coals of banksia bones, the bars of the *gradeja* tether the fish in its metal ribs, holding the flesh in place until it is cooked and falls apart, eat the crispy skin of the taylor and herring first, the sweetest meat by the tail, then eat carefully around the gut; careful, removing the thicket of bones. *Kupus* greens, potatoes, olive oil and garlic, paid for with the tail, fresh grilled from the shores of Korčula to the shores of Woodman's point, Coogee; eating the thicket of bones, tail flesh that dissolves, olive oil and garlic; whole green beans, the beans my *baba* picked with her own hands, piling into rusted tin cans and topping them with a wet hessian sack to keep cool while sitting on her verge waiting for the vendor to stop by and collect them for market; pickled red and green paprika with peppercorns and onion; the crispy fish skin of delight; *kruh*, a bone broth soup; the splintered bone shards of family. To think I'm eating the stomach, to think I'm eating my words, or the world, or the whole sea; *more more more* more – once, it was the sweetest thicket of meat by the tail.

Croatian–English translation
hrustule – a thin fried folded pastry, similar to Italian crostoli
gradeja – a hand-held stainless steel net mesh grill for cooking over coals
kiflici – a shortbread biscuit made in a crescent moon shape
kruh – bread
kupus – kale/collard greens
more – the sea
paprika – capsicum

Come Walk With Me

Come walk with me

           warm sunshine
                catch
    a dream

          you are not a flower

        my dandelion-
      beauty rare
        they   dig you up
      sweet as   butter

Fake Plastic Plants

Fake plastic plants, less trouble than the real ones,
Don't prickle or bite, need water or tenderness,
Nor love, nor whispered words to help them grow,
Only a breath or two to blow away the topsoil of dust.

Don't prickle or bite, need water or tenderness,
Flameless candles flicker a silicon chip breath,
Only a breath or two to blow away the topsoil of dust,
Never burn or blacken glass, nor get blown out.

Flameless candles flicker a silicon chip breath,
Like seedless watermelons they don't spit back,
Never burn or blacken glass, nor get blown out,
Or invoke the fear of sprouting plants in guts and ears.

Like seedless watermelons they don't spit back,
A dozen red roses, de-thorned, lacking scent, to wither,
Cannot invoke the fear of sprouting plants in guts and ears,
The lip-red gash, velvet petals beget the idea of a rose.

A dozen red roses, de-thorned, lacking scent, to wither,
Split hearts open, ocean to ocean every Valentine's Day,
The lip-red gash, velvet petals beget the idea of a rose –
A rose in name only without the sweet perfume reverie.

Splitting hearts open, ocean to ocean every Valentine's Day,
Salt of saccharin, sugar-free candy never lines the mouth,
A rose in name only without the sweet perfume reverie,
Sweeter than sweet – the tip of the tongue rapacious.

Salt of saccharin, sugar-free candy never lines the mouth,
Grandma's synthetic grapes don't lose their taste, chewy,
Sweeter than sweet – the tip of the tongue rapacious,
Fake plastic plants, less trouble than the real ones.

You Say Poetry is Dead

You say poetry is dead
as you sleep with your head
on the pillow of a bed in a sub-
urban nightmare –
'Black milk of daybreak we drink it at nightfall' –
with houses all the same-same,
houses and cul-de-sacs designed to confuse,
or is it a ruse to keep the thieves out
and the cars and the people in?
Did you ever think about the bars
on windows of urban homes, mothers
who can't leave, and mothers and fathers who must,
as their ankle bracelets beep, to feed
the open mouths of chicks who cheep cheep cheep,
and who work for the cheap clothes and shinies
made in China, consumed by consumers
with needs bigger than the wallets they
have to feed the mouths that cheep?
So we go round and round
the cul-de-sac of birth-work-taxes-death.

Poet. A false word, a lie, why? –
Say one thing, mean another, lie to your mother,
sister, father and brother – to get them to believe
that poetry does not breathe and fire
in every being, in every fibre, cell, atom, and neuron;
the tissue connecting your
mind and body like a verse.

The body itself is a poem, a building, a machine
look around: touch, move, breathe,
can you not see? I am not an illustrator,
yet everything I write is a facsimile,
a castle made of sand on the beach.
Things I see excite me and I want
to reproduce this feeling.
Did this poem make you *feel* anything?
Or did you shrug and go, 'Meh' –
this poet's making of her words is not for me
and you step with feet out into the world
and make your own poems and your own poetry:
frame frame frame, click click click,
'Look at me!' See?

We make our own stories
whether we want to or not
we are storied beings,
'Black milk of daybreak we drink you at nightfall…
drink you and drink you'
and drink you, until we fall into a sleep, deep
and milk-drunk as a newborn baby
to dream, 'What is poetry?'
A fugue in the burbs of dead-end streets,
a cat with a flea she cannot scratch,
an idea of a flame, an unlit match.

In the Night Wood

Tell a story

I've been hunting in the Night Wood

                            starving

    since before I was born,
  spent   days sleeping   in
the woods

a madness
      the beginning of a fairy tale,

                          recite some poetry

                                gather

my books

     lift my skirts

            return

                    to ground   .

My Body is a Poem

poems flow from my womb
like a wishbone
in waves
        in waves
                in waves

o o O

                        a fling

             a groan

             door opened
                        inside

  the

          fertile

O

Your Mother Says it Was the Books

Your mother says it was the books
'The books saved me,' I said.

I sat next to him   took his hand
touching him   embarrassed

smoke   ash
dissolve in his fingers
          like my — —
as we hid   pressed up against
the diamond web of the cyclone fence

      at the netball wind-up

          trouble
Your mother will never   forgive you

      a sinking feeling
a sigh.
narrow hallways
say good night.

a lie
'I never kissed him. Mrs XYZ is lying,'

because I knew
                    to touch my — — wasn't a sin
                and besides, why should I get in trouble?
I didn't — — him

Ornithology
In the hope that she will learn to fly

        tearful,

                throbbing,

                        kissed,

chilly

        letters

                inscribed

                              my real name

girl.

Mother Cento

From my mother's sadness, which was,
Tremulous breath at the end of my line,
I remembered her head bent towards my head.

She spends hours with her vegetables,
Her breath in mine, our fluent dipping knives –
These are the things she can count in her hands,

Emblems of perfect happiness
I can't confront.
How I loved those spiky suns
To scrawl on my tongue.

Mother, dear mother, the years have been long,
I'll bleach them and hang them in the sun,
A handful of paper ashes
To shelter you, my bird.

The First Drug

'It is permitted in a time of great danger to walk with the devil until you have crossed the bridge.' – Bulgarian proverb

the first drug I took / was home-made wine / at my parents' table
watered down / so little alcohol / it
looked like / three drops of blood / added to water

pressed / from Swan Valley grapes
bees clamouring for a / taste of the
pure saccharine intox / ication / and hope / left behind
(so many bees / tanked and groggy / we swatted them away like flies
later Dad said / they ruined the wine / made it go sour)

sugar added to the must / fermentation bubbled, frothed and /
hissed the *slačića* / into the deepest plumi-est pinkness /
the grape juice / smelt like the perfume
of an earth flower / growing in / oak barrels

then it was / tobacco / at six / on a dare
smoking butts / workers left behind / building our double-brick house in / Wattleup /
fags discarded / on a pile with chipped bricks / castoffs of pink insulation batts
that made you itch / if you touched them
Red Heads secreted / from my parents' green / everything drawer
I recall / the taste / a chemical bitterness
and a dirty breath / sucked from / the filter / before the stub / burnt out

I didn't smoke / a cigarette again / until I was / fifteen
on a dare / an older cousin / told me / I had to try it
everyone was doing it / and I ran down /
the dirt track / across the road
bush crackling / on either side / of me
spider orchids shivering / at my heavy strides
where the beehives / were hidden
so afraid / a swarm / would find me
I took two puffs / choked / then ran back home /
breathing into / my hands / to check the smell on my breath /
before Sunday lamb roast lunch / with the family

at seventeen / at a high school party /
we mixed scotch, vodka and Southern Comfort / into rocket fuel
boys lined up to / kiss my friend / against the fence / and feel her up
so drunk she could / hardly stand / and nobody thought /
it was strange / or to stop them / probably the same guys /

who said they hid in / a boy's closet / while he had sex / with a girl
so they could watch / she was a slut /
but he was not called / a name / he was just / a boy /

a north of the river school guy / we met at a sandstone uni party /
by the Swan River / told us 'don't drop acid' / he had a friend in
    the psych ward /
who freaked out / saw bees crawling out of the walls /
and people's eyes / even after he came down /
we passed on acid that night / and got blind drunk / instead

now I don't need / the devil's hand
– Bacchus held my hand – led me astray –
fed me blood / drop by drop / like a fledgling magpie /
when I was / crossing those bridges / sometimes / I still drink wine /
with a little bit of blood / and dirt / mixed in /
but I no longer run from bees

Bird Song

when I was   *old*

I lived

    found

      picked it up

        then I wrote

bird of song
  your voice is

Blue sky

    days   done

You lie under

        violet

Dear bird

As poets do.

Acknowledgements

Variations of these poems first appeared in the following journals:

82 Review (Issue 3.2): 'Come Walk with Me'

The Australian Multilingual Writing Project (Issue 2): 'Careful'

Australian Poetry Anthology (2018): 'Bird Song'

Australian Poetry Journal (Issue 7.2): 'I Hear Things'

Backstory Journal (Issue 6): 'How to Make Sand'

Bukker Tillibul (Vol. 8): an earlier version of 'Stories and Sand'

Creatrix (42): 'The Peppermint Tree'

Dream Pop! (Issue 2): 'ooO'

Fem Static Zine (Issue 5): 'Short Skirts'

Found Poetry Review (Vol. 10): 'Grains of Sand' and 'Dert Rendezvous' (republication)

Landscapes: the Journal of the International Centre for Landscape and Language (Vol. 9, Issue 1): '*Zemlja*' and 'Pioneer Day'

Southerly (Issue 78.2): 'No Box'

StylusLit (Issues 2 & 3): 'The Mouth is a Door' and 'Family History'

Tincture Journal (Issue 18): 'Dert Rendezvous' (first publication)

What Are Birds? (Issue 1.1): 'Mother Cento'

'First Blood: A Sestina' won the 2018 Bruce Dawe National Poetry Prize through the University of Southern Queensland.

'Bhreus' was awarded the Annette Cameron Award for an Unpublished WA Poet in the 2018 Katherine Susannah Pritchard Poetry Prize.

'First Blood: A Sestina' was awarded second prize in the 2017 Katherine Susannah Pritchard Poetry Prize.

'The First Drug' was commended in the 2017 Katherine Susannah Pritchard Poetry Prize.

References and Notes

'Domestic Life', 'Your Mother Says it was the Books', 'I'd See Patterns', 'Tell a Story', and 'In the Night Wood' were created, in part, using an erasure technique from pages in Susanna Moore's *The Life of Objects*, Knopf, 2012.

'Dert Rendezvous', 'My Little', 'Grains of Sand', 'ooO', 'Come Walk with Me', and 'Bird Song' were created using an erasure technique from pages in Emily Wright's *The Sands of My Life*, Tales of the Mojave Road Publishing Company, 1994.

'I Hear Things' was created using an erasure technique from Luis Alberto Urrea's *By the Lake of the Sleeping Children*, Anchor, 1996, p. 18.

'At a Girl' is an erasure of my own work, 'Educating a Girl'.

'Stories & Sand' references Cheryl Strayed's *Dear Sugar, The Rumpus Advice Column #48*: 'Write Like a Motherfucker' published online at *The Rumpus* in 2010; and Leonard Cohen's 'Anthem' from his album *The Future*, Columbia, 1992.

'Black Swan' is dedicated to those who fought, and continue to fight, for the preservation of the Beeliar Wetlands.

The definitions of 'wog' in 'Definition: Wog (n); A 'Thing' are referenced from David Wilton's 'Wog', *Word Myths: Debunking Linguistic Urban Legends*, Oxford University Press, 2004, pp. 95–96.

'You Say Poetry is Dead' references lines from Paul Celan's poem 'Fugue of Death'.

'Mother Cento' includes excerpts from these poems: 'Ending the Estrangement' by Ross Gay, 'Medusa' by Sylvia Plath, 'Clearances' by Seamus Heaney, 'A Practical Mom' by Amy Uyematsu, 'Mother, Summer, I' by Philip Larkin, 'A Dandelion for My Mother' by Jean Nordhaus, 'Rock Me to Sleep' by Elizabeth Chase Akers Allen, 'Not Here' by Jane Kenyon, 'The Great Blue Heron' by Carolyn Kizer, and 'To a Child' by Sophie Jewett.

Thanks

Firstly, I would like to acknowledge and pay my respects to the traditional owners of the land upon which I wrote this book, the Chumash of California; and to the Noongah of Western Australia, upon whose land the stories in these poems originated. I would like to express my heartfelt thanks to those who read early drafts of individual poems, or this manuscript: Beth Taylor-Schott, Emma Trelles, Michelle Detorie, Ellen Carey, Anne Dupee Chevitarese, Donna Cameron, Peter D-Napoleon, Daniel Young, and my classmates at Swinburne University. To the staff and administrators of the Bruce Dawe National Poetry Prize at the University of Southern Queensland – Meghann McGee, Professor Laurie Johnson and Professor Rhod McNeill – thank you for your support of my work. Thank you to the folks of the Santa Barbara writing community, especially Chryss Yost, George Yatchisin, Elaine Gale, Kimmie Dee, Cole Cohen and Amy Boutell. To the students at Santa Barbara City College who I work with at the Writing Center, your strength and determination to become better writers inspires me. To my Mum and Dad for the gift of a farm upbringing. And to my husband Brett Leigh Dicks, and son Samuel, you bring love, light and support for all things creative into my life.

www.ingramcontent.com/pod-product-compliance
Lightning Source LLC
Chambersburg PA
CBHW062152100526
44589CB00014B/1793